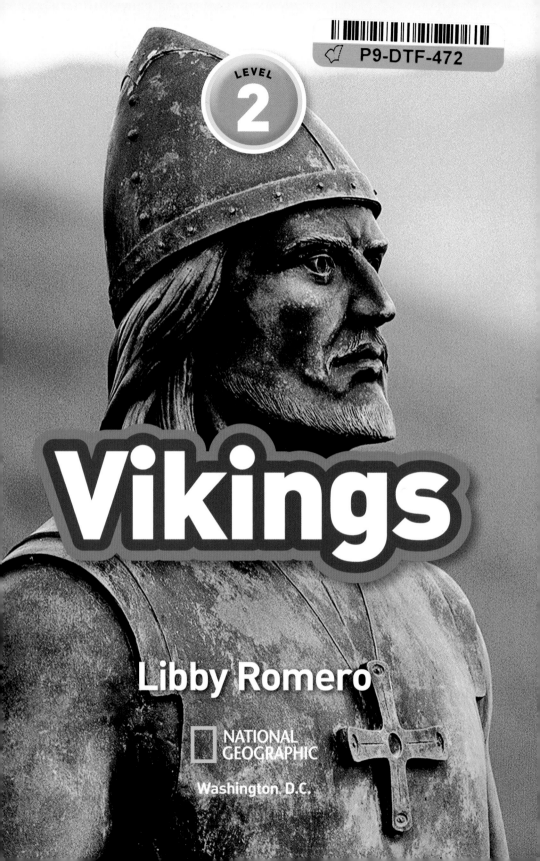

LEVEL
2

Vikings

Libby Romero

NATIONAL
GEOGRAPHIC

Washington, D.C.

For Jeff —L. R.

Designed by Yay! Design

Trade paperback ISBN: 978-1-4263-3218-0
Reinforced library binding ISBN:
978-1-4263-3219-7

The author and publisher gratefully acknowledge the expert content review of this book by Neil Price, Ph.D., chair of archaeology, Uppsala University, Uppsala, Sweden, and the literacy review of this book by Mariam Jean Dreher, professor of reading education, University of Maryland, College Park.

Author's Note

Vikings are interesting, but they aren't the easiest civilization to study. Artifacts are hard to find. Vikings built things out of wood and metal. And after a thousand years, wood rots and most metal rusts away. In fact, much of what we know about specific Viking people and events can be traced to Viking tales. These stories, or sagas, tell about epic battles and larger-than-life heroes. Fact or fiction, they provide some of the best clues we have about what it was really like to be a Viking.

Photo Credits

AL = Alamy Stock Photo; GI = Getty Images; NG = National Geographic Creative; SS = Shutterstock

Cover, Fernando G. Baptista/NG; vocab art, VectorPot/SS; header, Tribalium/SS;1, BMJ/SS; 3, Asmus Koefoed/SS; 4-5, Sam Kennedy; 5, Granger.com-All rights reserved; 7, Margaret Salter; 8-9, George Burba/SS; 8, Louis S. Glanzman/NG; 10 & 11 (UP, LO RT), Sisse Brimberg/NG; 11 (LO LE), CM Dixon/Print Collector/GI; 12-13, Danny Smythe/SS; 14-15, Tom Lovell/NG; 15, Louis S. Glanzman/NG; 16-17, Tom Lovell/NG; 18 (UP LE), Dmitri Mikitenko/SS; 18 (UP RT), Tom Lovell/NG; 18 (CTR LE), Jag_cz/SS; 18 (LO LE), Anna Jurkovska/SS; 18 (LO CTR, LO RT), Mny-Jhee/SS; 20 (UP), Walter Bibikow/GI; 20 (CTR), GTS Productions/SS; 20 (LO), Maarigard/Dorling Kindersley/GI; 21 (UP LE), RHIMAGE/SS; 21 (UP RT), Holmes Garden Photos/AL; 21 (CTR), Chronicle/AL; 21 (LO), Andrew J Shearer/iStock; 22, Sam Kennedy; 23, Leif Eriksson Discovers America (oil on canvas), Dahl, Hans (1849-1937)/Private Collection/Photo © O. Vaering/Bridgeman Images; 24 (LE), SvedOliver/SS; 24 (RT), Robert Harding Picture Library/NG; 25 (UP), Rue des Archives/Granger.com-All rights reserved; 25 (LO), ART Collection/AL; 26 (LE), Kevin Colin/EyeEm/GI; 26 (RT), Niklas Johansson/iStock; 27, Fotokostic/SS; 28, valeriiaarnaud/SS; 29, KEENPRESS/NG; 30 (UP), Gerry Embleton/North Wind Picture Archives; 30 (CTR), Doug Houghton/AL; 31 (UP LE), Leemage/UIG via GI; 31 (UP RT), Hervey Garret Smith/NG; 31 (LO LE), MattiaATH/SS; 31 (LO RT), Andrey Puzanov/AL; 32 (UP LE), Gerry Embleton/North Wind Picture Archives; 32 (UP RT), George Burba/SS; 32 (CTR LE), Leif Ericson sails past icebergs on his voyage to Newfoundland in c.1000 (color litho), English School, (20th century)/Private Collection/Peter Newark Historical Pictures/Bridgeman Images; 32 (CTR RT), Tom Lovell/NG; 32 (LO LE), Kevin Colin/EyeEm/GI; 32 (LO RT), Fotokostic/SS

National Geographic supports K–12 educators with ELA Common Core Resources. Visit natgeoed.org/commoncore for more information.

Printed in the United States of America
18/WOR/1

Table of Contents

Vikings Rule!

"Viking" is an old Norse word that means "pirate" or "raider." But when Vikings lived, most people called them Northmen, not Vikings.

When you think of Vikings, do you think of mighty warriors raiding a village? In movies and stories, that's often what we see.

Yet Vikings were farmers and sailors. They were explorers and traders. They made big boats and beautiful arts and crafts. And they told great stories, too. There is a lot to learn about Vikings!

decorated Viking sword hilt, or handle

Viking Life

Vikings came from what are now the countries of Norway, Sweden, and Denmark. They lived in many small villages.

Most villagers farmed and fished or worked as merchants and craftspeople. Other people were thralls, or slaves. Viking leaders called jarls (YARLS) ruled over many small villages. A powerful jarl sometimes became a king. The king controlled a larger area.

Viking Vocabulary

CRAFTSPEOPLE: People with special skills in creating arts or crafts, such as blacksmiths, jewelers, and shipbuilders

thrall

jarl

king

farmer

Most Vikings lived on small farms. They raised cattle, sheep, goats, and pigs. They grew food for the animals and people on the farm.

This illustration shows what it may have looked like inside a Viking longhouse. It was probably dark, crowded, and often smelly.

Several families and slaves lived together in a longhouse. Farm animals sometimes lived in the longhouse, too. This made it easy to care for the animals during the long, cold winters.

a longhouse in the L'Anse aux Meadows (LANTZ oh MED-ohs) National Historic Site in Newfoundland, Canada

Viking Vocabulary

LONGHOUSE: A long, narrow one-room building made of wood, stone, and grass

Arts and Crafts

Vikings were skilled craftspeople. They made jewelry out of metals and glass. They carved combs out of animal bones. They decorated their axes, swords, and shields. They turned everyday objects into works of art.

Viking silver

a gold jewelry box with Viking coins, silver beads, and jewelry

decorated gold jewelry

comb and case

11

Viking Ships

Vikings were also master shipbuilders. One kind of ship they built was a longship. Longships traveled fast and moved easily in the water. They carried lots of people.

Viking Vocabulary

LONGSHIP: A large, fast ship with a shallow bottom that Vikings used during attacks

RAID: A surprise attack

a model of a Viking longship

shields

rudder

Vikings used longships when they went on raids. They rowed the shallow boats right onto the beach. This made for a quick attack and easy escape.

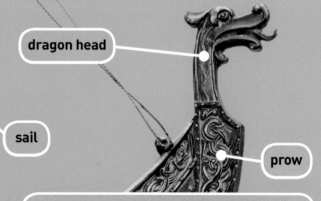

dragon head

sail

prow

Vikings sometimes carved figures such as dragon heads to put on the front of longships. The figures were meant to scare away evil sea monsters and spirits.

hull

In this painting, Vikings arrive in Newfoundland, Canada.

Vikings also built cargo ships. These ships were taller and wider than longships. They traveled slower and could carry more people. They could also sail up small rivers and across the ocean.

Vikings used these ships to explore distant lands. They filled the ships with goods that they traded along the way.

Vikings were expert sailors. They studied the sun, stars, waves, and birds. Even the color of ocean water helped them find their way.

In the Time of Vikings

During their time, Vikings were some of the most powerful people on Earth. Some Vikings raided churches and villages. They took supplies, money, and any valuables they could find. They captured people and kept them as slaves. Sometimes, they stayed to start a new Viking village.

Q Why did the Vikings cross the ocean?

A To get to the other side.

Vikings were some of the fiercest warriors in history. This painting illustrates a Viking raid.

fur

silk

In this painting, Vikings trade with Persian merchants.

spices

silver coin

Viking explorers and traders traveled by land and sea. They bought silks, silver, and spices. They sold iron, furs, honey, and wheat.

Some Vikings started towns where they traded. They became the first Europeans to live there.

Vikings traveled throughout Europe. They went to parts of Africa, Asia, and North America.

GREENLAND

ARCTIC OCEAN

ICELAND

NORWAY

SCANDINAVIA

←SWEDEN

RUSSIA

UNITED KINGDOM

IRELAND

←DENMARK

CANADA

Newfoundland

ATLANTIC OCEAN

EUROPE

UKRAINE

←FRANCE

NORTH AMERICA

Istanbul •(Constantinople) TURKEY

MAP KEY

→ Viking explorations

ASIA

The countries on this map are labeled with their modern-day names and boundaries.

AFRICA

SOUTH AMERICA

FACT or FICTION?

There are a lot of myths about Vikings. Can you tell which statements below are fact and which are fiction?

Viking men spent most of their time at war.

Fiction. Viking men spent most of their time working on their farms.

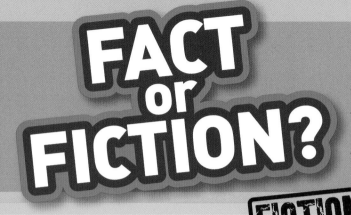

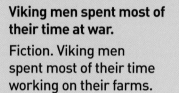

Vikings usually fought to settle arguments.

Fiction. Vikings believed in law and order. They created a system called the "Thing"— meetings where they made laws and gave out punishments. They settled arguments there, too.

Vikings buried some people in boats.

Fact. This was a great honor saved for the most important men and women.

Vikings wore helmets with horns on them.

Fiction. Vikings wore leather helmets with wood or metal frames. Horns would have gotten in the way during battle!

Vikings were tall people.

Fiction. Growing food was hard. Because of this, Viking children grew more slowly than kids do now. Viking adults were about three to four inches shorter than adults are today.

Viking women were powerful.

Fact. Viking women handled the family's home and money. They owned land, and some were fierce warriors. Recently, scientists proved that a high-ranking warrior buried in Sweden was a woman. Her grave contained weapons, armor, horses, and items used to plan battles.

Vikings were the first Europeans in North America.

Fact. They arrived in North America about 500 years before Christopher Columbus was even born.

Famous Vikings

There were many famous Vikings.
Here are some we remember today.

ERIK (AY-rick) THE RED: This red-headed Viking led a group of settlers to Greenland. They were the first people from Europe to live there. He named the big, icy island "Greenland" to attract more settlers.

FREYDIS ERIKSDOTTIR (FRAY-dees AY-ricks-DOTT-eer): She was Erik the Red's daughter. In some stories, she was a fearless warrior. In other stories, she was a lying, cheating murderer.

LEIF ERIKSSON (LAYF AY-ricks-son):
He was Erik the Red's son. He was the first European to explore mainland North America.

a painting of Leif Eriksson arriving on the shores of North America

Reykjavík (RAKE-yah-vik), Iceland, today

INGOLFUR and HALLVEIG ARNARSON (ING-olf-for and HAL-vayg ARN-ar-son): This husband and wife were the first Viking settlers in Iceland. They searched Iceland's coast for three years to find a place to settle. They picked an area now called Reykjavík. Today, this city is the capital of Iceland.

a statue of Ingolfur Arnarson in Reykjavík, Iceland

an illustration of Ragnar Lodbrok's raid on Paris in A.D. 845

RAGNAR LODBROK (RAG-nar LOTH-broke): He was a legendary Viking leader. He led many raids on England and France.

HARALD HARDRADA (HARR-ald Hard-RAR-da): This king of Norway is known as the last great Viking. He was killed in 1066 when he attacked England. Many call that battle the end of the time of Vikings.

a painting of Harald Hardrada's death

Discovering Vikings

Today, we learn about Vikings in different ways. One way is through their writings. Vikings carved messages in rocks, metal, and wood. They wrote in a language of letters and symbols called runes.

runes on wood pieces

runes carved into rock

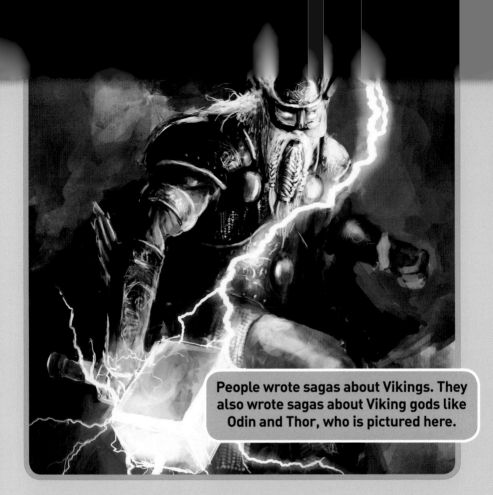

People wrote sagas about Vikings. They also wrote sagas about Viking gods like Odin and Thor, who is pictured here.

Vikings also told lots of stories.
These stories are called sagas.
In the 12th century, people started writing down the stories.

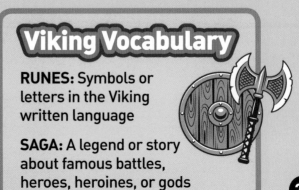

Viking Vocabulary

RUNES: Symbols or letters in the Viking written language

SAGA: A legend or story about famous battles, heroes, heroines, or gods

Sagas are more than great stories. They also have helped people find many Viking treasures.

People have discovered boats buried in the ground. They have found jewelry and weapons. They have even found parts of homes where Vikings first settled in North America.

This longship was found buried in Norway. It was discovered in 1904. That's about 900 years after the end of the time of Vikings.

In this photo, people act out the Battle of York, where the Vikings fought against the English.

Each discovery tells us more about Vikings and how they lived.

QUIZ WHIZ

How much do you know about Vikings? After reading this book, probably a lot! Take this quiz and find out.

Answers are at the bottom of page 31.

1

Which Vikings made jewelry and ships?

A. farmers
B. merchants
C. craftspeople
D. explorers

2

What were leaders of many small Viking villages called?

A. jarls
B. gods
C. thralls
D. kings

3

Where did Vikings originally come from?

A. Newfoundland, Greenland, and Iceland
B. Norway, Sweden, and Denmark
C. England, Ireland, and France
D. United States, Canada, and Mexico

4

What was on the front of some Viking longships?

A. a shield
B. a sail
C. a rudder
D. a dragon head

Viking traders bought _____ and _____.

A. silks and spices
B. honey and wheat
C. fur and iron
D. ships and jewelry

5

6

Which Viking was the first European to explore mainland North America?

A. Erik the Red
B. Leif Eriksson
C. Freydis Eriksdottir
D. Harald Hardrada

A rune is _____.

A. a story
B. a type of ship
C. a letter or symbol
D. a place

7

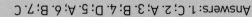

CRAFTSPEOPLE: People with special skills in creating arts or crafts, such as blacksmiths, jewelers, and shipbuilders

LONGHOUSE: A long, narrow one-room building made of wood, stone, and grass

LONGSHIP: A large, fast ship with a shallow bottom that Vikings used during attacks

RAID: A surprise attack

RUNES: Symbols or letters in the Viking written language

SAGA: A legend or story about famous battles, heroes, heroines, or gods